Western Australia

Land of Contrasts

NEW
HOLLAND

Western Australia

Land of Contrasts

LIZ BYRSKI

Published in Australia in 2001 by
New Holland Publishers (Australia) Pty Ltd
Sydney • Auckland • London • Cape Town

14 Aquatic Drive Frenchs Forest NSW 2086 Australia
218 Lake Road Northcote Auckland New Zealand
86 Edgware Road London W2 2EA United Kingdom
80 McKenzie Street Cape Town 8001 South Africa

10 9 8 7 6 5 4 3 2

National Library of Australia Cataloguing-in-Publication
Data:
  Byrski, Liz.
  Western Australia: land of contrasts
  ISBN 1 86436 321 5
  1. Western Australia - pictorial works. I. Title.

919.4100222

Publishing Manager: Anouska Good
Editors: Anna Sanders, Emma Wise
Design & cartography: Laurence Lemmon-Warde
Picture Researcher: Bronwyn Rennox
Design Assistant: Nicole Struik
Reproduction: Hirt & Carter Cape (Pty) Ltd
Printer: Tien Wah Press (Pte) Ltd, Singapore

PHOTOGRAPHIC CREDITS:
All photographs © Shaen Adey/NHIL with the exception
of the following: **Clay Bryce/Lochman Transparencies**:
p.49b; **Vicki Hastritch/NHIL**: pp 9, 104, 128t; **Anthony
Johnson/NHIL**: pp 14, 76t, 79b, 86, 87, 96b, 97; **Alex
Kayser**: front cover, half-title, title, pp 10tl, tr & bl, 12, 30t,
35, 36–7, 44–5, 46, 48, 51, 54–5, 57, 58, 60–1b, 70b, 72–3,
76b, 77, 78, 80, 81, 82–3, 84t, 88–9, 90, 91t & b, 92–3t, 92b,
93b, 94, 95, 102–3, 106–7, 110tl & r, 115, 117t, 128bl, 137b,
139; **NHIL**: pp 23b, 38, 42b, 43, 66b, 85; **Jaime Plaza Van
Roon/NHIL**: spine, pp 11br, 59, 63b, 65t, 79t, 108–9, 111t,
113, 130–31, 134, 142–43; **Geoff Taylor/Lochman
Transparencies**: p 49t & c.

Abbreviations; NHIL = New Holland Image Library
t = top, b = bottom, l = left, r = right, c = centre

HALF-TITLE Twisted trees, Karijini National Park.
TITLE PAGE Peaceful waters at Harold Bay; red dunes in
the Gascoyne; everlasting flowers in the Gascoyne.
THIS PAGE: Perth night skyline as seen from Kings Park.
FOLLOWING PAGE: The ancient and haunting landscape
of the Pinnacles, Nambung National Park, near Cervantes.

CONTENTS

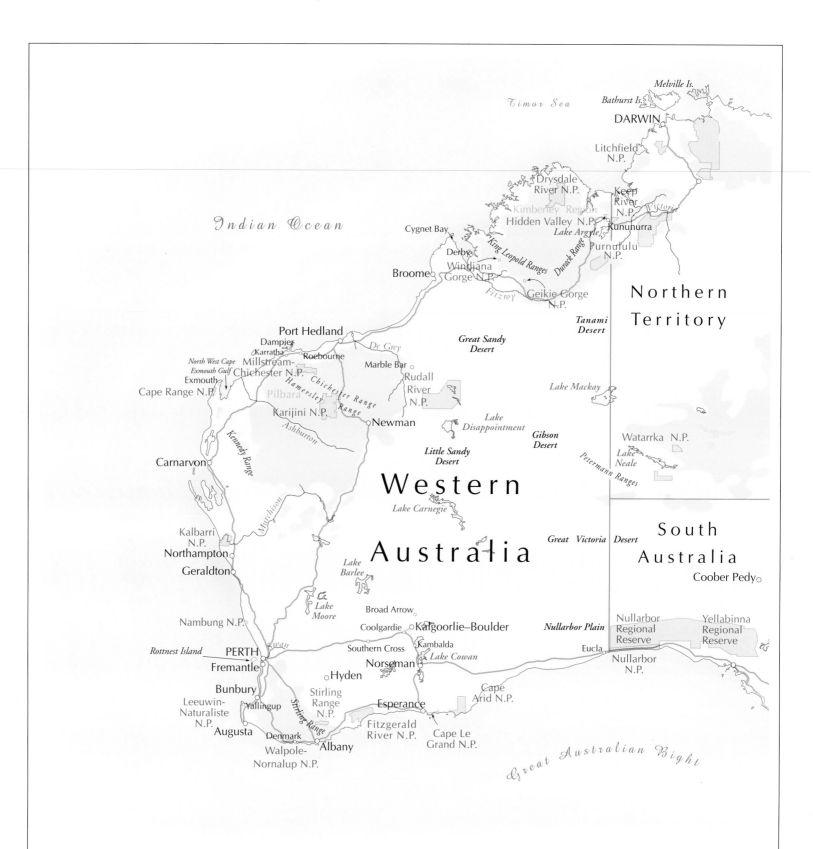

Timor Sea

Melville Is.

Bathurst Is.

DARWIN

Litchfield
N.P.

Drysdale
River N.P.

Keep
River
N.P.

Victoria

Indian Ocean

Kimberley Region

Hidden Valley N.P.

Lake Argyle

Kununurra

Cygnet Bay

King Leopold Ranges

Durack Range

Purnululu
N.P.

Derby

Windjana
Gorge N.P.

Broome

Fitzroy

Geikie Gorge
N.P.

**Northern
Territory**

*Tanami
Desert*

Port Hedland

Dampier

Karratha

Roebourne

De Grey

*Great Sandy
Desert*

North West Cape

Exmouth Gulf

Millstream-
Chichester N.P.

Marble Bar

Rudall
River
N.P.

Lake Mackay

Exmouth

Cape Range N.P.

Hamersley Range

Chichester Range

Pilbara

Ashburton

Karijini N.P.

Newman

*Lake
Disappointment*

*Gibson
Desert*

Watarrka N.P.

*Lake
Neale*

Kennedy Range

Carnarvon

*Little Sandy
Desert*

Western
Australia

Petermann Ranges

Murchison

Lake Carnegie

Kalbarri
N.P.

Northampton

Great Victoria Desert

South
Australia

Geraldton

*Lake
Barlee*

Coober Pedy

*Lake
Moore*

Nambung N.P.

Broad Arrow

Coolgardie

Kalgoorlie–Boulder

Nullarbor Plain

Nullarbor
Regional
Reserve

Yellabinna
Regional
Reserve

Rottnest Island

PERTH

Swan

Southern Cross

Kambalda

Lake Cowan

Eucla

Fremantle

Norseman

Nullarbor
N.P.

Bunbury

Hyden

Leeuwin-
Naturaliste
N.P.

Yallingup

Stirling Range

Stirling
Range
N.P.

Esperance

Cape
Arid N.P.

Augusta

Denmark

Fitzgerald
River N.P.

Cape Le
Grand N.P.

Walpole-
Nornalup N.P.

Albany

Great Australian Bight

N

Southern Ocean

A MESSAGE FROM THE MINISTER FOR TOURISM

The unique West Australian environment is rapidly emerging as a preferred destination for both domestic and international travellers seeking a nature-based tourism experience.

The pristine landscapes of Western Australia are beautifully complemented by many unique natural attractions, from the Bungle Bungle Ranges in the Kimberley, the coral reefs and whale sharks of Ningaloo, through the historic goldmining communities surrounding Kalgoorlie to the lush forests and pristine coastline of the southern region.

Western Australia is truly a natural paradise. It is also a state of diversity and hidden wonders waiting to be discovered.

A quality publication such as *Western Australia — Land of Contrasts* provides a spectacular overview of Western Australia's natural beauty and assists in understanding the state's unique attractions, regional centres and easygoing lifestyle.

I am sure you will enjoy reading this book as it showcases many of Western Australia's premier attractions and provides an insight into the relaxed lifestyle experienced in this fabulous state.

Norman Moore MLC
Minister for Tourism

ABOVE This kangaroo is on Lucky Bay Beach near Pemberton in the south of the state.

9

INTRODUCTION

From the tropical north to the cool, temperate southern forests, from glittering ocean beaches to wild and lonely inland deserts, Western Australia is a land of contrasts. The largest and most isolated state, this sprawling plateau of endless horizons occupies one-third of the continent of Australia. With its northern coastline only 10 degrees south of the equator, the state's vast size provides a backdrop to dramatic landscapes bathed in sparkling light — tropical swamps, massive gorges, rocky red outcrops, plains of waving wheat, rolling hills, vineyards, dazzling wildflowers, and cool, still forests woven through with sparkling streams and waterfalls. White beaches and rugged cliffs wrap the land on three faces through its 22 degrees of latitude, drawing a dazzling boundary with the Timor Sea and the Indian and Southern oceans. The eastern border is an arid desert of luminous sandhills.

Despite its size this is Australia's most sparsely populated state: just 1.8 million people, about 10 per cent of the nation's population, live here. More than 90 per cent of West Australians are situated in or around the capital city of Perth, the coastal plains and the fertile south-west corner of the state. The dry and lonely centre is largely uninhabited; its great distances and harsh climate making it hostile country for humans. Rich in natural resources and with a climate ranging from tropical to Mediterranean,

ABOVE LEFT The indomitable spirit of the West Australian outback abounds in its many hardy characters.
ABOVE RIGHT The billy's on for a mug of tea in the hot midday sun.
BELOW LEFT A common sight in the bush, rustic timbers fence a Pilbara farm.
BELOW RIGHT Old car wrecks acquire a ghostly dimension in the arid outback.

Western Australia is the most spectacular and diverse of Australia's states. Isolated from the rest of the country by deserts, it is a proud and independent land of tough, self-sufficient people with a fierce pride in their state's remoteness and difference.

HISTORY AND DEVELOPMENT

THE FIRST WEST AUSTRALIANS

Aboriginal people were the first to settle in this land, and evidence indicates that their occupation dates back more than 40 000 years. These first people made good use of the resources they discovered: native timbers were used to fashion weapons and utensils; and complex hunting and fishing systems, unique rock paintings, and food conjured from local flora and fauna were part of the culture of the first inhabitants. Ochre was mined and traded with people from as far away as the other side of the continent and visitors travelling south from Indonesia.

EUROPEAN SETTLEMENT

Dutch explorers were the first Europeans to make landfall and to map the west coast. In the early 17th century the Portuguese, English and French all reported sightings, but it was the English who first moved to colonise the country. A temporary military outpost was established at King George Sound in 1826 on a site which is now the harbour of the south coast town of Albany. In that same year Captain James Stirling sailed into the waters which are now Perth's Swan River and studied the lie of the land. Three years later he returned, bringing with him the first would-be colonists. On 18 June 1829 the Swan River Colony was proclaimed and the settlers waited impatiently on Garden Island, just off the coast, to take possession of their land.

As they unloaded their grand pianos, china cabinets and trunks of cumbersome, impractical clothing, the settlers had little

ABOVE LEFT Kangaroos can be found throughout Western Australia and are most likely to be seen at dawn and dusk.
ABOVE The Ord River Dam and Irrigation Scheme has opened up the north-east of the state to agriculture and industry.
BELOW LEFT A storm brews over Perth.
BELOW Western Australia's floral emblem is the Red and Green Kangaroo Paw.

idea of the life to which they had committed themselves. Surrounded by their possessions they huddled in tents in the sandhills until the land was allocated. There were hard times ahead — the climate with its searing summer heat and heavy winter rains, the lack of food, and the endless wait for supplies were only part of the

problem. They found the land was of poor quality, and unsuited to the sort of agriculture with which they were familiar. But the problems of the settlers seem insignificant when compared with the impact European settlement had on the indigenous population and, in particular, the southwest Nyoongah people.

THE CLASHES OF COLONISATION

Prior to colonisation Aboriginal people had lived successfully in small nomadic groups. A way of life which looked primitive to the settlers had been carefully adapted over thousands of years to suit the local conditions. The Aboriginal people were hunters and gatherers who lived in harmony with their environment, hunting and fishing only what they needed to survive. In the tradition of nomads they had no established homes and few possessions, moving across the country with the seasons. They supplemented their hunting with fruits, nuts and tubers, and covered themselves with animal skins. Aboriginal lifestyle and spirituality were intrinsically linked to the land, their religious rituals and ceremonies a vital part of their existence.

To Europeans, indigenous people did not appear to be cultivating the land. There were none of the familiar signs of settlement — no houses or domestic animals, no evidence of crops being planted or harvested. That Aboriginal people had prior ownership of the land and a vital affinity with it was not even considered, and when the Aboriginal people saw settlers killing their food source — kangaroos — and in their turn took cattle and sheep they were shot by outraged Europeans. Others were tricked and abused by the new occupants of their land or shot at for sport. In 1834, frustrated and enraged by the problems indigenous people presented to the colonists, Governor Stirling launched an expedition to wipe out the Nyoongah people, who by this time had started to form themselves into groups to resist the settlers' threat. Estimates of the number murdered vary between 50 and 200, and these were the youngest and fittest of the men. The survivors had no real alternative but to pledge allegiance to Stirling, and in the ensuing years European-borne diseases including tuberculosis, influenza, measles and whooping cough reduced the Aboriginal population even further.

THE CONVICTS ARRIVE

By the 1850s the Swan River Colony needed hard labour to assist its development. Transportation was, by this time, almost at an end in the eastern states, and the west requested its first draft of convicts. Many roads and public buildings in Perth, Fremantle and Albany are examples of convict labour and stand as reminders of a particularly brutal period in West Australian history. After their sentence was served the convicts obtained their 'ticket-of-leave' which allowed them to work for wages and gave them rights similar to those of the settlers. In all, more than 9000 convicts were transported to the Swan River Colony and made their homes there once they had obtained their ticket-of-leave.

GOLD!

Prosperity came with the discovery of gold in the north-west Kimberley region in 1885, and in the following years the Pilbara revealed more deposits of the precious metal. In the 1890s, a little further south, the goldfields area revealed more wealth and Kalgoorlie and Coolgardie emerged as the gold centres of the colony. Towns were established, only to be deserted a few years later when the gold was exhausted. Today the hot easterly winds pile the sand in shifting heaps on the verandahs and against the rotting timbers of the shops and houses of these eerie ghost towns. Only the Golden Mile of Kalgoorlie–Boulder has successfully continued mining operations, and Kalgoorlie remains a large and thriving oasis of life and activity in the wild and lonely reaches of the goldfields.

FEDERATION AND THE EARLY 20TH CENTURY

By the end of the 19th century Western Australia was a comfortable and independent colony with around 45 000 inhabitants. Many of the people working the land and running the colony had been born there and understood the land and the climate, and by 1900 the early pastoralists were driving large herds of cattle into the Kimberley. Although still seen as a poor relation by those on the eastern seaboard, Western Australia became one of the Federation of States in 1901.

Like the rest of the new nation, Western Australia moved into the 20th century cresting the wave of nationalism which followed Federation. Primary production was expanding at an encouraging rate, a small manufacturing industry was in its early stages and, off Broome, a healthy pearling industry was developing. While World War I took its toll on Western Australia — families lost their breadwinners and stations were run down — the state continued to grow. The railway arrived, as did commercial aviation, and the first suburbs between Perth and the bustling port of Fremantle developed. Western Australia continued taking shape with a period of steady growth which continued until World War II.

THE ECONOMY BOOMS

The postwar years brought great prosperity. The mining and export of iron ore grew and set the scene for an industry which today is a major contributor to the state's economy. Gold production at Kalgoorlie increased and coalmining in Collie fuelled the increase in electricity production and the railways. Transport and shipping networks were developed and expanded, and asbestos, copper and tin mining were also making their mark. Wool production soon doubled from its prewar level and wheat production remained consistent. In the mid 1950s the discovery of oil at Exmouth was another leap ahead.

The early postwar years brought a flood of European migrants to boost the state's workforce and economy. While migrants came to Australia from all over Europe, Italians and Greeks in particular settled in large numbers in Western Australia. In the areas surrounding Perth and through into the South-West, market gardens grew up along with citrus groves and orchards. While the first vineyards had been planted in the 1850s, postwar migrants contributed to a winemaking industry which today holds an important place in world wine markets. Western Australia was heading for

ABOVE The ore train delivers its precious load to Port Hedland on the Pilbara coast. OPPOSITE Built by the convicts it would later house, Fremantle Prison operated from 1855 until 1991 and is now a major point of interest for visitors to the city.

a bright future after World War II and at the end of the 20th century is still robustly fulfilling that promise.

WESTERN AUSTRALIA TODAY

THE ECONOMY

Today iron ore constitutes more than 20 per cent of Western Australia's export industry, followed by gold bullion at close to 18 per cent. The development of the petrochemical industry off the state's North-West Shelf has been a major contributor to Western Australia's growing economy and, since the discovery of diamonds at Lake Argyle on the Kimberley's Ord River, the state is now responsible for one-third of the world's production of diamonds. Wool, wheat and forestry remain vital factors in the state's diverse economic base. The fishing industry is now a major contributor, with West Australian rock lobsters, prawns and other seafood finding a huge market overseas, and the export of wine has increased dramatically in the last decade as the quality of the West Australian product has been recognised in European as well as Asian markets. Trade with Japan continues to be a dominant feature of the economy and Western Australia's other strongest export markets are China, the United States and Indonesia.

Exceptional growth has occurred in tourism in the last 20 years. With its magnificent scenery, spectacular beaches and

beaches, and stands against a backdrop of the richly wooded Darling Range and the winegrowing region of the Swan Valley. The Swan River itself is a focal point of the city with its busily chugging ferries, flotillas of sailing boats and windsurfers whipping across the glittering waters on refreshing breezes from the Indian Ocean. A spacious and elegant cultural precinct houses the Western Australian Museum, the Art Gallery of Western Australia and the State Library,

FREMANTLE AND ROTTNEST ISLAND

Close to the capital, the busy port city of Fremantle, with historic buildings, colourful markets and pavement coffee shops, is an added attraction. Just 19 kilometres off the coast of Fremantle is Rottnest Island which was originally established as a prison for Aboriginal people from the mainland. Rottnest is now a haven for those wishing to escape the mainland's bustle. Attractions such as magnificent beaches, rocky walking

abundant sunshine, the state is becoming a favoured destination for tourists from around Australia and the world.

PERTH

Perth, the capital of Western Australia, stands on the Swan and Canning rivers — the site of Governor Stirling's establishment of the Swan River Colony. A sparkling and vibrant city, it boasts some of the state's finest

and from here a plethora of small galleries and cultural venues fan out into Northbridge — the city's restaurant and cafe centre, and the heart of Perth's busy nightlife. Perth's history is mirrored in its buildings — from the early convict constructions through periods of art deco and art nouveau to the postwar developments of brutalism and modernism, and the massive towers of glittering glass and iron erected in the last 20 years.

ABOVE The sun sets on Perth — the world's most isolated capital city.
OPPOSITE Western Australia is home to over 400 species of reptiles.

tracks and cyclepaths, low-cost self-catering accommodation and the almost total absence of motor vehicles make it a year-round favourite for family holidays.

A STUNNING NATURAL ENVIRONMENT

To truly experience Western Australia, its extraordinary sense of space and dramatic contrasts, it is essential to venture outside Perth and its environs, taking time to explore the many faces of this diverse land — north, south and inland. The sheer size of Western Australia, its richness of colour and texture and the diversity of its flora and fauna imbue its landscapes with a magic and mystery all its own. Cavernous gorges, stony plains, towering forests, and red deserts are as much a part of this state as peaceful bays with silver beaches, stark white salt flats, and dazzling acres of wildflowers.

FLORA

Western Australia is home to at least half the continent's 30 000 plant species, and many thousands of these are unique to the state. The wildflowers which bloom between April and October spring to life with the first winter rains, carpeting the state with breathtaking colour from north to south. Kangaroo paws, boronia and Geraldton wax plants fill the bush with colour, while the pink, yellow and russet of the banksia, the spiny red bottlebrush and the brilliant yellow of the Cootamundra wattle are among the best known of more than 8000 species of flowering plants.

In the South-West forests karri trees more than 90 metres high tower majestically above sturdy jarrah and tingle trees. The dense, rich forest floor teems with insect, animal and bird life. Windswept plains dotted with spinifex; rambling bush where the spines of ancient grasstrees fan out in eerie, spiky globes; and the fruit-laden citrus trees and carefully trimmed grape vines combine to create Western Australia's breathtaking floral landscape.

FAUNA

Kangaroos and wallabies are common in Western Australia, with western grey and

red kangaroos most often seen at dawn and sunset. The sudden sight of a pair of emus is sure to delight, while possums, wombats and many other small nocturnal species can be spotted in the bush, the forests, the plains and rocky outcrops. Western Australia also boasts some unique species, the best known being the quokkas found only on Rottnest Island.

The coastal waters of Western Australia are home to whale sharks, sea lions and dugongs; and dolphins are a common site frolicking in west coast waters. They are particularly prevalent off Bunbury and in the waters of Monkey Mia in Denham Sound where they often swim alongside humans in the shallows. Humpback whales are regular visitors and southern right whales, once hunted almost to extinction, are slowly returning to West Australian waters. In the northern waters fresh and saltwater crocodiles stalk their prey and marine turtles slip silently onto the beaches and islands.

Crocodiles are not the only cold-blooded creatures in Western Australia — more than 400 species of reptiles are found in the state, many of them in the vast inland deserts. Dragon-like goannas and blue-tongued bobtails are easiest to spot, while frill-necked lizards and thorny devils merge cunningly into rocks and bush, darting from the sound of human intrusion.

More than 500 bird species are found in Western Australia, from vivid and noisy parrots and cockatoos, to kookaburras, eagles and osprey. The stately black swans which live in and around the Swan and Avon rivers have become a characteristic symbol for the state.

CLIMATE

The climate of Western Australia varies widely because of the sheer vastness of the state. In the tropical north the summers are hot and wet — temperatures rest most of the time above 35°C and are frequently well up into the 40s. The warm, dry winters in this region bring delightful days in the low 30s and comfortably cool nights. While occasional tropical cyclones can bring high winds and heavy rain to the north, the inland deserts and semi-desert regions are endlessly dry with Marble Bar and Eucla believed to be the hottest locations in Australia!

The south of Western Australia enjoys a delightful climate with long, hot summer days in the low 30s, peaking to the high 30s in January and February. July is the heart of winter but daytime temperatures rarely fall below 10°C and nights only occasionally drop to around 5°C. This area gets most of its rain between May and August. Travelling further south to the coast, the winds and storms of the Southern Ocean moderate the summer heat and increase the winter rainfall.

LIVING IN THE LAND OF CONTRASTS

Western Australia has often been called the 'Lucky State' in the 'Lucky Country'. While business and industry hum with the pressure of international trade and commerce, the outstanding climate and Western Australia's distance from the rest of Australia's centres of population have bred a relaxed lifestyle all its own. Australian Rules Football in

winter and cricket in summer are hugely popular as participant and spectator sports, as are netball, tee ball and volleyball. Surfing, windsurfing, skindiving, sailing, canoeing and bushwalking are also very popular weekend activities.

Food is always a good indicator of the nature of a society and the West Australian menu reflects the state's multiculturalism with a diversity of tastes to delight any palate. While barbecues and picnics still rate highly, outstanding local wines and locally made beers complement a truly international cuisine — one result of

Western Australia's rich and diverse ethnic mix. As Australia moves towards becoming a republic, old ties to Britain are becoming less relevant and a variety of European and Asian rituals and ceremonies are the focus of celebrations in Western Australia's towns and cities. While the war years brought an increased influence from the United States, this has been diluted in recent times. An increased emphasis on Western Australia's proximity to Asia and its future as a trading partner and neighbour has challenged West Australians to consider the nature of their state in relation to South-East Asia.

ABOVE Beautiful dawn hues on popular Rottnest Island which offers a magical retreat from the mainland and city life.

The visual and performing arts have thrived in recent years and multiculturalism can be witnessed in all its diversity. Galleries, art exhibitions and sculpture can be found throughout the state's cities and towns. Live theatre, opera, dance, classical and international music can be enjoyed in Perth and other major cities, and innovative

touring plans bring many aspects of the performing arts to smaller and more remote locations throughout the state. Aboriginal culture — including art, music and dance — is increasingly valued by the broader community and a number of West Australian Aboriginal performers are making a significant impact on the international arts scene. The annual Festival of Perth provides a rich collection of international performances and exhibitions which often include major installations and lively street theatre.

It is more than 150 years since the first white settlers began destroying Aboriginal culture and, driving the people from their land. The Aboriginal population of Western Australia was more than halved in the early years of settlement; but despite slaughter, disease and dispossession, the state's indigenous people have survived. Protesters rallied against outdated laws in the late 1940s but it was the 1960s and 1970s before there was any significant shift in attitude towards Aboriginal people. In 1993 federal legislation acknowledged the right of indigenous people to the use of their land and debunked the concept of *terra nullius*. Reconciliation between Aboriginal and non-

Aboriginal Australians and the conservation of the spectacular but fragile environment, combined with the need for economic development and expansion, are major challenges which West Australians must confront as they move into the 21st century.

Contrast and diversity are key features of Western Australia's landscape, climate, history, community and lifestyle. This land of contrasts, which has played a leading role in the nation's economic development and international status, offers a welcome as warm and broad as its landscapes to visitors from all corners of the world.

The Kimberley

*F*or tens of thousands of years Aboriginal people trekked through the wild and remote Kimberley, but this last frontier of Australia's north-west has defied most other attempts to explore its many mysteries. This is the top end of Western Australia, bounded by the Indian Ocean and the Timor Sea, with a coastline of massive sandstone cliffs, submerged reefs, and mangroves which form a barrier to exploration from the north. To the south an arbitrary boundary created by the Fitzroy River separates the Kimberley from the rust-red dunes of the Great Sandy Desert, and eastwards the Ord River and its valley run close to the Northern Territory border. There are more than 270 000 square kilometres of this vast and magical wilderness, where breathtaking scenery is painted in dazzling colours by the clarity of the light, the seemingly endless sunshine and the torrential winter rains.

The Kimberley is one of the oldest landmasses in the world, having emerged from the sea over 2500 million years ago. Englishman William Dampier, in his efforts to chart the north and west coasts of the continent as a passenger on the ship *Cygnet*, made landfall in 1688 in what is today known as Cygnet Bay, near the Dampier Peninsula. But it was a land expedition headed by Alexander Forrest in 1879 which led to the initial settlement of the Kimberley. Forrest encouraged the grazing of sheep and cattle, and soon drovers from New South Wales and Queensland were taking huge herds across long and arduous trails to the north-west.

A townsite was proclaimed at Derby in 1883 and a wooden jetty was built there

two years later, ensuring the development of the town's port. The discovery of gold at Halls Creek in the same year signalled the start of Western Australia's first, albeit short-lived, gold rush. Today the mining tradition continues, with the Argyle Diamond Mine producing up to 35 per cent of the world's diamonds, among them the rare pink, champagne, cognac and fine white stones.

While Derby is now the busiest town of the region — Australia's first airmail service was born in the Kimberley with the first flight between Derby and Perth in 1921 — and Wyndham is an important port, Broome, on the south-west edge of the Kimberley, is the most popular centre for visitors to the region. Just 18 degrees south of the equator, this thriving town was once the leading centre of the world's pearling industry. Broome has a rich Aboriginal history and a colourful community influenced by the Japanese, Chinese and other races attracted there in the early days of pearling.

Vast beaches fringed with palm trees, sparkling blue water, endless sunshine, a lively arts and music scene, and colourful festivals make this a haven for tourists.

Life in the Kimberley is dominated by the climatic extremes of the Wet and Dry. Between December and March there is a hot summer of monsoonal rains and minimum temperatures rarely dropping below 34°C at night and daytime highs soaring above 40°C. The summer rains swell the rivers and creeks, making many roads impassable and isolating small towns and cattle stations. This is the time when the varied and colourful flora of the Kimberley bursts spectacularly into life almost overnight against a background of awesome torrents, raging rivers, waterfalls, and electrical storms. The Dry begins in April, peaking in July and although temperatures ease a little they rarely fall below 35°C in the daytime, with evening temperatures more comfortable and less humid than in the Wet.

The Kimberley's striking geology is created by a massive fossilised marine coral reef system which dates back 350 million years to the Devonian period. The remains of this ancient reef lie between the Indian Ocean and the Fitzroy River, and the most spectacular examples are at Geikie Gorge on the Fitzroy and Windjana Gorge on the Lennard River. The stunning rock faces have been carved by time and the elements into craggy promontories, cavernous inlets and pitted honeycomb. Massive 90-metre limestone cliffs splashed with vivid colours — cream to golden yellow through to orange and deep red, silver to steel grey and purple through to green and black — are dazzlingly mirrored in the river waters.

Dating back to the same period, the Bungle Bungle Range stands on a plateau more than 200 metres above the surrounding plain. These huge beehive-shaped forms are striped in the rich orange of siliceous sandstone and the greenish-black of algae. This unique natural wonder was known only to the indigenous Kija and Jaru people, and some pastoralists, until it was 'discovered' in 1983 by a television crew flying over the area.

The Kimberley is rich in the Aboriginal history of the Dreamtime — creation stories in which ancestral spirits roamed the lands creating natural features and establishing rituals and laws. The Great Kangaroo Marlu, the Wandjina and the Maletji Dogs are the spirits of the Kimberley; and some of the most ancient and spectacular rock paintings in the world — the Wandjina

paintings at Panda–Goornnya and other examples at Kalumburu, the Oscar and Carr Boyd ranges, and the King Edward, Glenelg and Napier rivers — are evidence of the rich cultural life of the Kimberley's indigenous people.

The vegetation and wildlife of the Kimberley region contribute to its mysterious character. Giant melaleucas and bare, bleached weeping paperbarks, freshwater crocodiles basking on fossiliferous rocks, and fruit-eating bats clustered on mangrove branches seem to have been there since the beginning of time. Kingfishers, parrots and sulphur-crested cockatoos chatter in the trees, and herons and cormorants dry their wings at the water's edge. Skinks and bobtailed lizards dart through cracks in the rock face or lie watchful and motionless in the silence of

PREVIOUS PAGES AND ABOVE The beehive-shaped domes of Purnululu (better known as the Bungle Bungles) rise from a massive plateau more than 200 metres above the surrounding plain.

the gorges. Overhead a wedge-tailed eagle scours the parched earth for a rabbit or small bird. Most distinctive in the Kimberley landscape are the boab trees which are found only in the far north of Australia and are closely related to the African baobab. With their smooth bulbous trunks and branches like great gnarled fingers reaching to the sky, each tree seems to have a character of its own.

Remote, wild and rich with life, the Kimberley is a panoply of Western Australia's most extraordinary contrasts.

ABOVE During the Wet the Lennard River roars through the Windjana Gorge. During the Dry it is reduced to a series of waterholes.

RIGHT Growing up to five metres in length, fearsome saltwater crocodiles inhabit waterways throughout northern Australia. They have been known to kill humans, horses and livestock.

OPPOSITE Tunnel Creek is a kilometre long natural tunnel through the Oscar Range. It served as a hideout for legendary Aboriginal outlaw Jandamarra late last century.

ABOVE AND BELOW From the wild inland ranges to its mouth at the Cambridge Gulf, the Ord River is vital to life in the Kimberley. The precious waters of the Ord are now trapped by the Ord River Dam and Irrigation Scheme to irrigate vast areas of the north-east Kimberley. The scheme opened up the region to a variety of agricultural crops including soya beans, bananas, sunflowers, maize, beans, cucumbers and melons. LEFT Established in 1960 as the base for the Ord River Irrigation Project, Kununurra has since become the administrative centre of the region's thriving agricultural community.

ABOVE Towering more than 12 metres above the waters of the Fitzroy River, the multi-coloured cliffs of Geikie Gorge are a wonderland of caves and tunnels carved by the river and flood waters which sweep through the gorge in the Wet.
FOLLOWING PAGES The dazzling turquoise waters off Gantheaume Point are just one of the attractions which have turned Broome into a thriving tourist centre.

LEFT Whether swimming, riding camels or fishing, the magic of Cable Beach captures the imagination of tourists and locals.

OPPOSITE Nestling behind palm-fringed beaches, the thriving town of Broome is home to many local artists and craftspeople whose work is displayed in the picturesque shops.

BELOW Bathed in the rose-gold glow of sunset, the camel trains head homeward along Cable Beach.

THE PEARLS OF BROOME

Pearling began in the waters off Broome late in the 19th century and by 1910 the town was the leading pearling centre in the world. More than 3500 of the town's 5000 inhabitants were engaged in the industry and more than 350 luggers worked the area. Most of the first divers were Aboriginal but when the European fleet owners moved in, men from the Asia–Pacific countries replaced the locals. As the industry grew, Chinese and Japanese traders established themselves in the town.

In those early days pearl shells for mother-of-pearl were in greatest demand and Broome supplied 75 per cent of the world market. In 1914, with the start of World War I, many luggers were requisitioned and around this time some of the first synthetic mother-of-pearl was produced, destroying the market. The industry continued with more emphasis on natural pearls but this was dealt another blow when the Japanese divers, believed to be the best in world, left the region with the onset of World War II. Broome might have become a ghost town were it not for a revival in the demand for cultured pearls in the mid 1950s, when the first pearl farms were established.

Pearling was a difficult and dangerous job and in the early days many divers perished from the 'bends' — the painful formation of nitrogen in the blood caused by rapid surfacing. Storms and cyclones, a feature of this area of the Indian Ocean, also took their toll.

Some truly spectacular pearls have been found off Broome. The 'Southern Cross', for example, a shell containing nine pearls shaped like a crucifix, sold for $48 000 to the Vatican collection.

Today the Broome pearl industry is smaller but it still has an outstanding international reputation for the quality, variety and the sheer beauty of its pearls.

BELOW Lake Argyle, formed by the Ord River Dam and Irrigation Scheme, is Australia's largest artificial lake. The famous Argyle Diamond Mine is located nearby.

ABOVE Nicknamed the Walls of China, these naturally formed limestone walls, which run for several kilometres near Halls Creek, look more like human handiwork than nature's own creation.

BELOW AND OPPOSITE Squat and bulbous or elegantly cylindrical, boab trees *(Adansonia gregorii)* are a unique feature of the Kimberley landscape. The Prison Tree, near Derby, was used as an overnight lock-up in the early days of the colony.

The Pilbara

The Pilbara is an ancient land — ironstone country — a place of rocky outcrops and dusty red ranges, a primordial landscape of endless horizons. This parched and stony terrain is even older than the limestone of the Kimberley and is one of the hottest places on earth. Beginning west of the Great Sandy Desert, the Pilbara incorporates the stunning peaks and troughs of the Hamersley Range and some of the richest mineral-producing country in Australia. From its red-hot centre it stretches westwards to include the glorious Coral Coast which, with its world famous Ningaloo Reef, unique marine life, flora and fauna and magnificent climate, is a much favoured destination for ecotourists.

The Pilbara is also the focus of Western Australia's mining industry. The iron ore and natural gas produced here are both major sources of the state's wealth. The mining towns and ports are thriving centres of population and the inland mine sites are intense pockets of labour and industry.

It seems an extraordinary contradiction that the parched plateaus dotted with spinifex and the scorched plains where the earth cracks in the heat grew from the ocean floor more than two billion years ago. The land is pockmarked with great fissures and gorges which plunge deep into the iron-rich sandstone. This is one of the lowest rainfall areas in Western Australia, with the extreme summer heat rising to the high 40s and evening winter temperatures dropping to zero. Along the north and

PREVIOUS PAGES The mineral-rich red land of Karijini National Park is in the heart of the Pilbara.
LEFT Spectacular gorges are to be found throughout the vast Hamersley Range.
FOLLOWING PAGES Spinifex, rock and sand create a breathtaking vista along the great sweep of the Hamersley Range.

Coral coasts, the winters are the most enjoyable time of the year with daytime temperatures of around 28 to 30°C.

Many of the descendants of the original pastoralists still work the Pilbara properties and other vast areas have been opened up since the early days. A number of small, busy towns developed, particularly along the coast, with places such as Port Hedland and Cossack becoming important ports of entry for essential supplies, vital outlets for the export of gold and copper, and satellite centres of the flourishing pearling industry in Broome. At the height of the gold rush, gold was discovered at Marble Bar and well over 100 mine sites operated in the area.

The Burrup Peninsula near Dampier on the north coast is the point at which gas from the massive natural gas fields of the North West Shelf is piped ashore to the onshore treatment plant for liquefaction or onward piping elsewhere for export. The Burrup Peninsula is also the site of some of the world's most spectacular and prolific prehistoric rock art which depicts a variety of native wildlife.

The other major peninsula of the region is the North West Cape, located between Onslow and Coral Bay — a large extension of land enclosing the Exmouth Gulf. Until recently a secret US Navy communications base was located at the tip of the cape, and in World War II a refuelling base for American submarines was sited near Wapet Creek on the gulf. Today the North West Cape is an extremely popular region for ecotourism with a stunning array of land-based wildlife as well as the spectacular marine life at the Ningaloo Reef Marine Park. The richness and diversity of flora and

fauna in the Cape Range National Park, which extends the length of the cape, equals that of the marine life on the reef. Large rusty-grey wallaroos called euros gather to graze in large groups on the coastal land. Ospreys, kites and honey-eaters can be found here, in addition to a myriad other bird species breeding and nesting in this exceptional wildlife haven.

The wildlife and flora of the Pilbara varies across the region with four major national parks of outstanding beauty, each well endowed with a huge range of native plants, birds, mammals, insects and reptiles. Wondrous gorges, still pools and the stark white trunks of red river gums with their soft green foliage stand in sharp contrast to rocky plains. In the Wet, cascading waterfalls and rocks covered in verdant moss create cool oases. Eagles and bustards, crows and emus, and a variety of small tits and finches, white cockatoos, pink galahs and parrots cluster in the trees while majestic pelicans can be seen

making their stately landings on the waters of the coastal inlets. On the rocky plains and in the bush, dingoes, feral cats, and some foxes hunt their prey and the native echidna makes its home.

The Pilbara's major town and port is Port Hedland which, thanks to the iron ore boom, is one of Western Australia's fastest growing towns with many new suburbs built to accommodate the increasing numbers of workers in the region's mineral fields. Salt is another big factor in the region's economy. In fact, in excess of 2.5 million tonnes of salt is exported from the Pilbara every year, harvested from around Port Hedland and Dampier. Karratha is another town which is mushrooming in size to accommodate the needs of the natural gas and iron industries. The nearby town of Cossack was the first north-west port — a pearling centre and the place where camels were loaded to transport supplies to inland cattle stations. Many of the original buildings from the end of the last century have since been lovingly restored and maintained. Likewise Roebourne, about 40 kilometres inland, is the site of many fine examples of late 19th century architecture and building. Many of the Pilbara's urban centres are newer mining company towns — Tom Price, Newman, Dampier, Pannawonica and Paraburdoo, among others, have all grown from the needs of the mining industry and are well equipped to cope with the isolated locations and the extreme climatic conditions.

The rugged Pilbara landscape is distinctly different from other parts of Western Australia, and the rest of Australia, and its vast mineral resources make it one of the richest regions in the country.

TOP Some of the finest and most unusual Aboriginal rock paintings in Australia are to be found in the Pilbara.

ABOVE A myriad colours and textures combine to create the ancient mosaic that is the rock face of Hamersley Gorge.

RIGHT A rock pool in Karijini National Park. Karijini is the second-largest national park in Western Australia and is now managed jointly by the original indigenous owners of the land.

FOLLOWING PAGES Purple mulla mulla throws a carpet of colour across the Pilbara landscape. The delicate, papery flowers are swathed with downy hairs giving them a soft and cloudy quality.

TOP AND ABOVE White snappy gums abound in the Pilbara, giving the region around the 200 000-hectare Millstream–Chichester National Park an internationally recognised 'outback' look. Spinifex, snappy gums and the characteristic mineral-rich red Pilbara dirt give a good indication of the intensity and dryness of the heat of the Dry season. LEFT The Pilbara bushland, parched and cracked by the summer heat, softens to a floodplain with the first rains. Like much of the harsh West Australian landscape, the region springs to life after the rains and teems with wildlife and wildflowers.

NINGALOO REEF

Ningaloo Reef, which extends for 260 kilometres along the North West Cape, is a smaller version of the Great Barrier Reef, and is the remains of a vast reef structure dating back more than 15 million years to the time when the north-west of Australia was covered by a shallow sea. Today the area is a protected marine park with sanctuary zones where the extraordinarily wide range of marine life can be seen in all its varied and intricate beauty. More than 220 species of coral flourish at Ningaloo, with each spawning season laying the foundations for further reef growth.

The reef is extremely accessible, lying close to the shore and in some places only about 100 metres from the beaches. The area between reef and shore is a joy for snorkellers and skindivers with magical underwater scenery alive with hundreds of thousands of tiny fish in glittering shoals darting in and out of the colourful and crustacean-rich reef formations.

Along the pristine beaches of the North West Cape, green-back turtles move silently ashore to lay their eggs, while whale sharks inhabit the deeper waters off the reef around Exmouth. These large and gentle creatures are the largest fish in the world, growing up to 18 metres in length. Feeding on small fish and plankton, they pose no threat to human beings. In June and July humpback whales can be seen as they make their way northwards to the calving grounds off the Montebello Islands.

In 1994 the West Australian Government introduced legislation to protect this unique location from oil drilling; the sanctuary zones also protect areas of the reef from fishing in order that this stunning natural wonder may continue to be a safe haven for numerous marine species.

OPPOSITE AND TOP Ningaloo Reef, protected by the Ningaloo Reef Marine Park, stretches over 4000 square kilometres. At times only 100 metres offshore, Ningaloo Reef is tantalisingly close to the Pilbara coastline for diving enthusiasts.
ABOVE Diving with the massive but harmless whale sharks is just one of the attractions for visitors from around the globe.

RIGHT Cossack was the main port for the region at the end of the last century. Now a ghost town, some of its original buildings, including Galbraith's Store (c.1891), have recently been restored.

ABOVE The town of Roebourne was the main administrative centre for this region at the end of the last century.

RIGHT The Pilbara is the home of the iron ore industry which amounts to more than 20 per cent of Western Australia's exports.

OPPOSITE Natural gas from the North West Shelf is piped to shore at Dampier for both domestic use and international export.

The Gascoyne and
the Mid-West

In the waters which wash Australia's coastline lie the wrecks of the many ships lost in these perilous seas. Many explorers, seafarers and adventurers from Europe, attempting to chart the coast or make landfall, lost their lives off Western Australia's coast, south of North West Cape. The stretch of coast which runs down from the cape to the mouth of the Moore River has a history of shipwrecks which exceeds any other section of the coast. Looking at the colourful and dramatic coastal gorges, and the vividly banded cliffs rising hundreds of metres above the crashing waves of the Indian Ocean, it is easy to understand how this spectacularly beautiful coastal scenery would have attracted the early seafarers, drawing them towards fatally turbulent and rocky waters. The Mid-West coast, from the mouth of the Gascoyne River, south to the port city of Geraldton and past the gentle curves and beaches to Moore River, is an area of outstanding scenic and historical interest. Dazzling shell beaches and curving sandy shores, still and sheltered coves, craggy cliffs and tiny historic fishing villages form the coastal fringe of a region also famed for its magnificent wildflowers.

The inland climate is very hot with most rain falling in the winter, and evening temperatures more comfortable than the tropical heat of the north-west. Along the coast, however, the climate is particularly beautiful — warm and dry and with its major city, Geraldton, boasting the title 'Sun City' for its average of eight hours of sunshine per day throughout the year. But this coast is not only a haven for sun seekers.

Surfers, skindivers, anglers and underwater explorers flock to the region. The glorious coast, within reach of some of the most spectacular areas of wildflowers in the state, make tourism an important factor in the economy of the Gascoyne and the Mid-West. Sheep and cattle farming also rank highly, with almost a quarter of Western Australia's grain harvest, fat lambs, wool, pigs and beef being produced in this region.

Mining is also on the increase here as are the lucrative lobster and crayfishing industries.

The Gascoyne River flows from rocky inland heights towards the thriving town of Carnarvon with its beautiful beaches and banana plantations, and opens into an estuary where pelicans gather and the coastal waters teem with scallops and prawns. A few hundred kilometres south at Shark Bay, Monkey Mia's famous dolphins swim alongside humans, playing and rolling in the water as they make their daily visits to the beach. The gentle and entertaining

creatures draw tourists like a magnet. Nearby in the sparkling turquoise waters of Hamelin Pool, stromatolites — bulbous toadstool-like formations — stand up to half a metre high at low tide. These ancient life forms have evolved over 3500 million years and are created from sediment trapped in algae which slowly, in a daily process of photosynthesis, forms and hardens. Varying in colour from black through shades of grey and sandy beige, and splashed with orange, they are grouped thickly at the water's edge.

South of the Peron Peninsula the towering Zuytdorp Cliffs lead down to the town of Kalbarri and the long white beaches at the mouth of the Murchison River. Here in the magnificent Kalbarri National Park the stunning gorges of the Murchison River open to vast sweeping slopes of wildflowers and endless vistas of banksias which tinge the horizon with tones of yellow, orange and red.

About 60 kilometres off the coast lie the 108 islands of the Abrolhos archipelago — the centre of an expanding crayfishing industry. The island reefs are a wonderland of marine life and the many species of birds, reptiles and rare small mammals found on the islands make them magical wildlife havens. South of Geraldton's thriving port and industrial centre, the coast is dotted with a number of small historic coastal towns and hamlets where beautifully restored stone buildings shelter under the spreading branches of ancient trees dotted with chattering parrots and cockatoos.

From the coast to the inland areas, this region boasts the greatest profusion of wildflowers in the 'Wildflower State'. Moving inland it seems that the landscape is carpeted with colour — vibrant yellows and reds, rich blues and purples, and the whites and pinks of the dainty everlasting flowers. At ground level, and in the multitude of richly flowering trees, the dazzling variety of floral species creates a springtime spectacle which never fails to enchant both locals and visitors to the region.

Fittingly in this state of dramatic contrasts, where flora and fauna abound, the starkness and mystery of the desert is not far away. In the heart of the Nambung National Park, the Pinnacles Desert stands, its sharp and craggy limestone pillars and knobs protruding from the sand. Believed to be the fossilised root systems of some of the forbears of the dense coastal heath plants which surround Nambung, the Pinnacles form one of Australia's most haunting landscapes.

Further inland, the Gascoyne and Mid-West farms give way to wheat lands and cattle stations, to flint and granite, and the beginnings of the wild red interior landscapes which lead to the goldfields.

PREVIOUS PAGES The Gascoyne is splashed with colour almost overnight when fields of everlasting flowers burst into bloom after the first rains.
BELOW Dating back 3500 million years, the 'living rocks' or stromatolites in Hamelin Pool are the world's second-oldest known fossil.

LEFT   From its source at Peak Hill the Murchison River meanders for 80 kilometres through the steep gorges of Kalbarri National Park.

BELOW   Named after botanist Sir Joseph Banks, who accompanied Captain Cook on his journey to Australia, banksias can be found in every Australian state but are more prevalent in Western Australia where there are more than 40 endemic species.

OPPOSITE The cool blue waters of the Little Lagoon at Shark Bay are fed by the sea via a tidal creek.
RIGHT In the sparkling waters of Monkey Mia, playful and friendly dolphins socialise with the visitors who travel huge distances to swim alongside these gentle intelligent creatures. Dolphins were first spotted visiting the bay more than 30 years ago.
BELOW They may look clumsy but these pelicans are graceful and dignified in flight and are a regular sight along the magnificent Kalbarri beaches.

ABOVE Loop Bend — twisting and turning through the Kalbarri National Park, the Murchison River has taken two million years to cut deep gorges through the sandstone.
RIGHT Nature's Window forms a natural rock frame for a stunning view of the Murchison Gorge in Kalbarri National Park.
OPPOSITE Hawks Head, named for the shape of its jutting rocks, is a splendid vantage point for viewing some of Kalbarri's finest landscapes.

BELOW The towering Zuytdorp Cliffs rise to a height of more than 170 metres above sea level. This stretch of coast was the downfall of many early explorers and seafarers whose wrecked vessels rest beneath the waters of its rocky shores.

THE 'WILDFLOWER STATE'

Not for nothing has Western Australia been called the 'Wildflower State'. Wherever you go and at almost any time of the year some of the state's more than 8000 species of flowers and flowering trees will be in bloom, but in late winter and spring in the Gascoyne and Mid-West the spectacular variety and beauty of the state's flora is truly breathtaking.

Western Australia's floral emblem is the kangaroo paw and in the Gascoyne and Mid-West the many varieties flower in profusion, from black with greenish-black leaves curling around white blooms to the better known deeply coloured red kangaroo paw. Western Australia is also home to 46 of the almost 60 species of banksia in Australia. Some of the finest displays of these nuggetty trees with their large, colourful blooms are to be found in Kalbarri National Park. As the Murchison River cuts through the park's magnificent gorges, the flaming reds and oranges of the banksias bloom in profusion over the hills and valleys along with more than 500 species of flowering plants including red, yellow and white grevilleas, and white and purple star flowers.

The region is also home to some of the finest of Western Australia's 300 species of native orchids, as well as carpets of dainty everlasting flowers, so-called because the papery flowers retain their shape and colour when dried. These delicate daisy-shaped flowers appear after the first rains, growing densely in great expanses of pink and white.

The vastness of the West Australian landscape, combined with the dense growth of flowers and flowering trees, make unbelievably colourful vistas a feature throughout the state. Even in areas where the land seems too dry to sustain any growth, the first rains bring forth a dramatic burst of dazzling blooms.

ABOVE Rough seas, forced at great pressure through holes in the rock, send water jets shooting up to 20 metres high at the Blowholes, north of Carnarvon. Large waves and king tides are an everpresent danger and have been known to sweep spectators into the surf.

FOLLOWING PAGES The mysterious landscape of the Pinnacles Desert, near Cervantes. These strange calcified spires of limestone have been exposed by tens of thousands of years of erosion. Early Europeans thought they had discovered the remains of an ancient city.

ABOVE The treacherous Kalbarri coastline is the result of millions of years of pounding surf and howling winds. Close examination shows layers of iron deposits — another indication of Western Australia's great mineral wealth!

RIGHT A grader works on smoothing the salt pan at Carnarvon, on the coast of the Gascoyne. More than 1.5 million tonnes of salt are produced each year at Lake MacLeod.

OPPOSITE Millions upon millions of minute white shells piled more than 10 metres deep make up the dazzling brilliance of Shell Beach, near Denham. The shells are packed so tightly that they can actually be cut into blocks and used as building materials.

Perth and its Environs

More than 40 000 years ago Aboriginal people were the first inhabitants of the land on which the city of Perth, its suburbs and the port city of Fremantle now stand, and for the surviving Nyoongah people this land has strong spiritual links to the Dreamtime and their ancestral spirits. Willem de Vlamingh and his men were the first Europeans to land here in 1696, and de Vlamingh named the river 'Swan' after the rare black swans which lived there. The Swan River Colony was founded by Captain James Stirling 133 years later.

Today Perth is a vibrant city, as well as an important commercial centre and the capital of a state which is a leader in the Australian economy. Almost 1.5 million people, 80 per cent of the population of Western Australia, live in and around Perth — the most isolated state capital in the world, and the gateway to what has been dubbed the 'State of Excitement'.

In the heart of the city, steel and glass skyscrapers constructed during the boom of the 1980s stand alongside elegant 19th-century buildings. A sophisticated business district, a spacious and elegant cultural centre, first-rate shopping, theatres and cinemas, as well as a lively and colourful restaurant and club scene in the Northbridge district, cater for every need. On the edge of the city, the prestigious University of Western Australia stands in sunlit grounds fringed with ancient shady trees; its theatres, courtyards and open-air cinema are venues for many of the events

PREVIOUS PAGES Facing the city skyline, these catamarans, lined up on the fore-shore at South Perth, will soon be skimming across the waters of the Swan River.
LEFT The juxtaposition of architectural styles brings an interesting dimension to the Perth central business district.

in the annual Festival of Perth. This feast of cultural activity incorporates art, drama, dance, music, street theatre and associated events from around the world.

Pride of the city is Kings Park — a four-square-kilometre park which sweeps across Mt Eliza providing stunning views across the city and river to the foothills of the Darling Range. Kings Park combines areas of natural bush with cultivated native parkland and a 17-hectare botanical garden displaying 2000 species of West Australian plants. Walking tracks and cyclepaths, avenues of tall shady trees, narrow creeks of sparkling water and sloping lawns surrounded by exotic native plants make Kings Park a perennial favourite for locals and tourists. Nearby, the impressive West Australian Parliament House, its brace of slim and sparkling fountains catching the sunlight, faces down the long sweep of St Georges Terrace, the heart of Perth's business district.

The route north to Yanchep passes splendid beaches where surfers cluster in patient groups waiting for the next wave. Kangaroos, wallabies and emus wander confidently through the Yanchep National Park, the tree-tops alive with the cries of colourful parrots, cockatoos and kookaburras, and a wide variety of waterbirds gathering at the lake. Although not native to Western Australia, koalas can be seen here perched sleepily in the eucalyptus trees. The park also has a network of fascinating limestone caves and passages.

When Captain Stirling first landed in Western Australia he took a particular liking to the Swan Valley and it is easy to see why he was enchanted. The fertile pastures and woodlands in the foothills of the Darling

Range are spectacularly beautiful. Carpeted with wildflowers in the spring and lushly green in winter, the area now also boasts vistas of citrus groves and vineyards.

South-west of Perth, at the mouth of the Swan River, lies the working port city of Fremantle. Proudly multicultural, the rich ethnic mix of the Fremantle community is reflected in the diversity of restaurants, cafes, colourful festivals and entertainment.

It is also a popular centre for visual and performance artists. The famous Fremantle Markets, established in 1897, are a weekly attraction selling everything from food to clothes, jewellery and artworks.

Some of the state's most historic buildings can be found in Fremantle. Overlooking the neat curve of Bathers Beach, the 12-sided limestone Round House, the state's first public building and originally a prison, dates back to 1831. On the other side of town, Fremantle Prison was built by convicts in the early 1850s and, close by,

the original Warders' Cottages have been lovingly restored, and the town's arts centre and museum are housed in a magnificent limestone building which was once the lunatic asylum. The Maritime Museum has an international reputation for its maritime historical research in a state where so much history and present-day activity is focused on the coastal regions. Fremantle was the location of the 1987 America's Cup defence and is a favourite location for leisure yachting.

Just 19 kilometres off the coast is the glorious Rottnest Island with its turquoise waters, perfect beaches and fascinating reefs. Its beauty belies its dark history — the early settlers established Rottnest in 1838 as a prison for Aboriginal people. With no concept of the nomadic nature of Aboriginal life and scant respect for indigenous people, the European settlers incarcerated mainland Aboriginal people on Rottnest for taking sheep or pigs, defending their territory, and other crimes of survival essential to their lifestyle. Accessible by sea or air, Rottnest is just five kilometres wide and 11 kilometres long, and motor transport is restricted to essential services. Quiet walks, cycling, swimming and skin-diving are some of the favourite activities at Rottnest, along with evenings under the trees feeding the friendly local quokkas, and regular visits to the bakery as its aromas waft temptingly around the island.

Despite its significance as a major centre in the South-East Asian region and its major role in the nation's economy, Perth's sun-soaked days, dazzling blue skies, and the nearby waters of the Indian Ocean, create a relaxed sense of the good life which is relished by West Australians.

RIGHT The vista of suburbs, which stretch almost 50 kilometres north, provides a background for the tall buildings of Perth's city centre.

BOTTOM Bicycles are the best way to enjoy the narrow winding paths and shady tree-lined avenues of Kings Park.

BELOW Shopping or just browsing is a favoured pastime in Perth.

ABOVE Honouring West Australians who died defending their country, the War Memorial in Kings Park stands proudly against the backdrop of the Swan River.

BELOW Western Australia's oldest and most prestigious seat of learning — the University of Western Australia — is located on the edge of the city at Nedlands.

LEFT As well as spectacular views of Perth, Kings Park boasts a 17-hectare botanic garden, an array of the state's wildflowers and a vast area of natural bush.

ABOVE   Landmark Norfolk pines back Perth's favoured Cottesloe Beach and frame the traditional grace and charm of the restored Indiana Teahouse.

OPPOSITE   This aerial view of riverside residences in the prestigious suburb of Dalkeith gives a bird's-eye view of the 'lifestyles of the rich and famous'. These houses are, or have been, owned by some of Western Australia's most famous or infamous millionaires.

FOLLOWING PAGES   A tranquil lake and sparkling fountains provide a counterpoint to the busy working life of Western Australia's capital city.

ABOVE Graceful in bronze as in nature — black swans form the focus of the fountain at the Burswood Island Resort which is home to Perth's international casino.

OPPOSITE A cameo of Tudor England in the heart of Perth. Picturesque London Court is packed with tiny jewellery, antique and novelty shops. In the window of the clock tower St George relentlessly fights the dragon every 15 minutes.

LEFT Perth's warm climate and long summer days allow visitors and residents a relaxed outdoor lifestyle.

LEFT Meandering through the centre of Perth, the beautifully serene Swan River is an essential part of the city's lifestyle.

BELOW The famous black swans (*Cygnus atratus*) with their red eyes and bills are Western Australia's fauna emblem and can be found in thriving colonies on many lakes and waterways.

BELOW The night is young. A favoured location in Fremantle's lively nightlife —
the old Freemasons Hotel built in 1854 has been restored and enlarged, and is
now the popular Sail and Anchor Hotel, home of locally brewed beers. On the
opposite corner is the original Fremantle Markets, established in 1897 and a
perennial favourite for avid shoppers searching for bargains.

TOP High Street at sunset. Many of Fremantle's beautiful buildings owe their existence to the sweated labour of the convicts who began to arrive in the colony after 1850.

ABOVE Heading off into the sunset, the liner *QEII* leaves Fremantle harbour.

LEFT Fremantle's famous Round House stands at the end of High Street. This is the state's oldest building, dating back to 1831. Originally a prison, it was used to house Aboriginal people before transportation to the Rottnest Island prison.

ABOVE A riot of action and colour, the annual Fremantle Festival draws the crowds.
RIGHT These street performers entertain passers-by inside the Fremantle Markets.
OPPOSITE A hearty breakfast, or just a cup of coffee — Fremantle's 'cappuccino strip' is always popular.

ABOVE   A fireboat in the Fremantle harbour. Fremantle has been a busy
working port, servicing the capital, Perth, for more than 150 years.
OPPOSITE A perfect replica of the *Endeavour*, which brought Captain James
Cook to Australian shores in 1770, was built in Fremantle and set out from
here on her maiden around-the-world voyage.

ABOVE The view of Fremantle from the Round House, showing the city's many colonial buildings and emphasising its substantial colonial past.
OPPOSITE The magnificent *Endeavour* replica in Fremantle harbour.
BELOW One of Fremantle's four harbours. Very much a port city, Fremantle played host to Australia's unsuccessful 1987 America's Cup defence.

BELOW Just 19 kilometres from the mainland, Rottnest Island, with its white beaches, peaceful bays and sparkling clear water, is a paradise for holiday makers.

ABOVE Fish Hoek Bay, Rottnest Island. Paradise is an island just 11 kilometres long and five kilometres wide. Laze in the sun, ride a bike or take a trip in the glass-bottomed boat over sparkling, clear waters. RIGHT Cars are banned on Rottnest Island, so bicycles are the perfect form of transport. LEFT With so many magical bays to choose from, you can find a beautiful beach in any direction on Rottnest Island.

ROTTNEST'S UNIQUE QUOKKAS

When Dutch navigator Willem de Vlamingh made landfall at Cottesloe on the West Australian coast in 1696 he also paid a visit to a nearby island. There he was surprised by the large number of small animals which he mistook for rats. De Vlamingh accordingly named the island Rottnest (Rat's Nest).

The creatures which de Vlamingh saw were quokkas (*Setonis brachyurus*) — small, bounding marsupials about the size of a cat. It is estimated that there are in excess of 8000 quokkas on the island and that this is now the only place they can be found, although there is an opinion that a few may still be living in some of the state's South-West forests. About half a metre in height with a tail almost 30 centimetres long, the quokka's fur is brown and grey, tinged with rust on the top and silvery-grey on the belly.

Today the Rottnest quokkas are one of the island's major attractions. They can be seen almost everywhere, wandering around the grounds of the holiday cottages and into the central square at Thompsons Bay. They have adapted to the growing presence of visitors on the island and many will confidently approach humans, looking up expectantly for a hand offering some food. It is common for holiday makers to open the cottage door in the morning to find a quokka or two on the back step looking hopefully for a sign that the remains of breakfast may be coming their way. But the best time to see quokkas is at dusk when they emerge in greater numbers.

Quokkas are endearing, cuddly-looking creatures which are, on the whole, extremely friendly, but they will deliver a sharp nip to the disrespectful human attempting to catch them!

The South-West

$\mathcal{D}$eep in the cool green heart of the southern forests, where the early morning mists rise to reveal waterfalls sparkling white with foam and still, rock-studded pools reflect the myriad colours of the trees, it is hard to believe one is in the same country as the vast red horizons of the Pilbara or the windswept ghost towns of the goldfields. The South-West is a fertile land of rolling green hills, vineyards, orchards and small farms. Thriving little towns and hamlets, glorious bays of white sand backed by rugged cliffs, fertile pastures with grazing cattle and dense woodland where the tall trees rise amid massive clumps of wild white lilies, make this a favoured corner of Western Australia. The vast size of the state means that to get anywhere on land involves long journeys through huge uninhabited areas broken only by the sight of a roadhouse or distant isolated rural property. But the South-West, while large, is a compact and more densely populated area. Here roads weave through pretty villages and small towns, and narrow side roads wind off to little farms, wineries or clusters of rammed earth cottages — beautifully restored heritage buildings where visitors can enjoy mulled wine and open fires in winter and grilled local trout with chilled white wine in summer.

The South-West enjoys the most moderate climate in the whole of Western Australia — warm summers where the temperatures rest around the low 30s and cool winters where

PREVIOUS PAGES Cape Naturaliste in the state's South-West corner boasts some of the region's finest coastal scenery. Its many rocky headlands are also the perfect viewing points for watching humpback and southern right whales.

LEFT The forests of the South-West contain some of the tallest trees in the world, including these tingle trees.

soft rains are interspersed with days of dazzling winter sunshine and clear blue skies. Swimming, surfing, fishing, horse riding and bushwalking attract visitors from within the state, the east and overseas, while the less active can wander through the craft shops, potteries and art galleries, or weave their way through the wineries tasting the local product. Only a few hours drive from Perth the South-West has an extremely successful tourism industry which includes first-rate accommodation and restaurants where fresh local fish, fruit and wines top the menus.

Just 70 kilometres from Perth the growing coastal town of Mandurah is an increasingly popular resort with its beautiful beaches and the waters of the Peel Inlet providing seemingly inexhaustible crabbing and prawning. The major town of the region is Bunbury — the second-largest town in the state and an important port and business centre. Gracious old buildings sit alongside the newer areas of the town with ease and, like Monkey Mia, Bunbury is blessed with regular visits from bottlenose dolphins, always a great attraction for visitors. Busselton, situated on the long inlet of Geographe Bay, is a lively and relaxed town with glorious and safe sandy beaches and shady coves.

The coast sweeps up into a jagged corner which runs from Cape Naturaliste to the southern point of Cape Leeuwin where the waters of the Indian and Southern oceans meet. The beaches along this stretch of coast are a mix of white and golden sands and rocky inlets with some of the finest surfing conditions in the state. Yallingup, with an international reputation for its

waves, also boasts a huge network of stunning and beautiful underground caves.

A little further inland the town of Margaret River has developed as the centre of the winegrowing region. This pretty and prosperous town is fast becoming a haven for artists and craftspeople whose work is displayed in the many local galleries. Lavender, berries and soft fruit are grown at many of the surrounding properties. The

wineries in the Margaret River region are a great deal more than just vistas of well-trimmed vines. Most offer wine-tasting facilities and many have first-rate restaurants and craft galleries or potteries. In recent years wine production in the area has grown to meet an increasing demand as the local product has attracted widespread interest and acclaim both in Australia and overseas — there are now more than 40 wineries in this comparatively small area.

South of the winegrowing region is timber country, and the forests of the

South-West are breathtaking. Massive forests of tall jarrah, marri, and tingle rise to extraordinary heights but tallest of all are the karri trees, some reaching a height of more than 90 metres. The forests which surround the logging town of Pemberton are particularly beautiful with the forest floor alive with the rustle and movement of small mammals, insects and reptiles, and the treetops noisy with kookaburras, parrots, lorikeets and honey-eaters. Kangaroos and emus emerge at dawn and sunset from their homes deep in the woodland, and the fast-flowing rivers and streams are home to local trout and waterbirds. Logging is big business in this region with many small towns relying entirely on the timber industry for their existence.

Along the southern coast, where the massive cliffs and pristine beaches are washed by the waters of the Southern Ocean, the climate, cooled by the ocean winds, is particularly pleasant. At Augusta, where the Blackwood River opens to the sea, flocks of gulls and large stately pelicans cluster in the shallows, and along the coast towards the tiny town of Denmark rocky inlets and tiny bays are backed by sweeping hills and distant forests. The landscape here can change dramatically from still and peaceful blue waters and smooth granite rocks baked by the sun to wild lashing waves and surf against the steely grey backdrop of the stormy Southern Ocean sky.

The rich and fertile pastures, forests and vineyards of the South-West are dramatically different from most other regions of the state, creating yet another dimension to this land of spectacular contrasts.

ABOVE Breathtaking in its natural beauty, Bunker Bay is one of the many magical inlets along the broad sweep of Geographe Bay at Dunsborough.
FOLLOWING PAGES The southern coasts of Western Australia are world-renowned for their stunning surf beaches. Margaret River is the scene of one of Australia's major surfing carnivals.

OPPOSITE LEFT Frogs are one of the many species to be found in the cool moist depths of the South-West forests.

OPPOSITE RIGHT Keeping a lookout. A pair of grey kangaroos checks out the situation before emerging from the bush.

RIGHT A unique perspective on the South-West's majestic tall trees can be gained from the remarkable treetop walk through the Valley of the Giants.

BELOW Giant hardwood karri trees are a feature of the South-West forests and are the third-tallest hardwood trees in the world.

RIGHT The beautiful southern coast of Western Australia, near Denmark, was once a major site for Australia's whaling industry — with up to 850 whales killed per season. These gentle sea giants quickly returned to the southern coast after the last whaling station closed in nearby Albany in 1978.

THE SPECTACULAR UNDERGROUND WORLD

From Cape Naturaliste to Cape Leeuwin the spectacular beauty of the South-West coast is matched by pockets of unique underground scenery. The extensive network of limestone caves in this region has been formed by the action of rainwater, carbonic acid and decomposed plant matter dissolving the limestone to leave groups of caves tens of thousands of years old. In the underground chambers and passages of the Yallingup, Jewel, Lake and Mammoth caves, exotic formations and fossil remains create a glistening wonderland of unearthly shapes and patterns.

The limestone formations in these caves are outstandingly beautiful, with colours ranging from purest white through gold, orange and rust to purple and steel grey. Some hang like great curtains of gathered fabric while others, fine and lacy, drape in delicate folds like the finest shawl. Seemingly from another world, ancient and beautiful shapes and colours are reflected in the glassy still waters of underwater lakes and pools rippled only by the occasional chill drop of water.

Fossil remains found here have provided much information about the species which inhabited these regions in prehistoric times. The fossilised jawbone of a giant wombat-like creature was found at Mammoth Cave, and Jewel Cave was the site of the discovery of fossil remains of a Tasmanian Tiger. Tiny marine creatures, insects and traces of mammals are all here, frozen in delicate fossilised beauty.

Some of the stalagmites and stalactites in the South-West caves are the largest in the world, and huge chambers have been carefully lit to display these spectacular formations to their greatest advantage. The raw chill of the atmosphere and the haunting beauty of the limestone shapes and colours are an experience not to be missed. In addition to these caves, which are open to the public, many others in the region are accessible to experienced spelunkers.

ABOVE Miles of sand and some of the finest swimming you could wish for make the
coast of Geographe Bay one of Western Australia's most favoured holiday locations.

LEFT AND BELOW Wine barrels at a Margaret River winery and vineyards near Yallingup. A thriving wine industry has grown up in the South-West region and many local wines have made their mark on the domestic and international markets.

OPPOSITE A favourite location for surfers, the glorious Yallingup Beach is a focus for the lively and picturesque little town clustered on the hillside above.

The Great Southern
and the Wheatbelt

etween the semi-desert of the goldfields and the rich, fertile pastures and forests of the South-West, the wild and craggy coastline and wooded ranges of the Great Southern stretch eastwards to the fringes of the Nullarbor Plain and northwards to the wide horizons and endless wheat fields of the Wheatbelt. Along the south coast with its huge, soaring cliffs, the Southern Ocean winds bring a climate which is cooler in summer than the South-West and distinctly colder in winter, but long, warm summer days are still a feature of the region. The coastal stretch, particularly between Albany and Esperance, is a collection of rocky bays backed by huge cliffs and sandy beaches where salmon are landed and southern right whales can be seen both close to the coast and on a short boat trip out from King George Sound.

The town of Albany was established in 1826, three and a half years before Perth, as a military encampment. Later its fine harbour made it the ideal site for a whaling port and then a coal loading station for ships heading to the eastern states. This beautiful location was originally occupied by Aborigines and much evidence of their occupation can be found in the area, particularly at Oyster Bay.

The deep blue waters off the coast and the magnificent King George Sound with its green and rocky islets and many sandy beaches provide a surrounding landscape of exceptional charm and beauty.

The town of Esperance was first settled in the 1860s but it was gold which established

PREVIOUS PAGES Endless fields of wheat produce a massive crop which is an important commodity in the state's economy.
LEFT Albany, formerly a thriving centre of the whaling industry, is a lively coastal town with many reminders of its colonial history, including its civic buildings.

the town as a port. It is now a thriving agricultural centre and the area is popular with tourists for its spectacular beaches, coastal scenery and a climate which, while sun soaked, is considerably cooler than many of the state's other resorts. Nearby, the more than 100 tiny islands of the Archipelago of the Recherche are home to a huge variety of waterbirds as well as colonies of seals and penguins.

The Great Southern has some fine national parks, including the magnificent Cape le Grande with its tranquil beaches and granite cliffs. The isolated coastal Cape Arid National Park is a favourite location for bushwalkers and birdwatchers because of the many varieties of wildlife to be seen, from flocks of wild geese to frolicking seals. Fitzgerald River National Park is one of the state's finest locations for wildflowers with more than 70 species of wild orchids unique to this region. Honey possums, tammar wallabies and endangered dibblers can be found here along with a wide variety of other animals.

Further inland the Stirling and Porongorup ranges, which are carpeted in spring with more than 500 varieties of wildflowers, enclose a rich agricultural region. The Porongorup Range is the oldest volcanic range in the world with landscapes of green slopes, granite outcrops and spectacular stands of karri. The Stirling Range with its own unique wildflowers and stark granite peaks blending from grey to purple is, like the Porongorup Range, magical country for walkers and rock climbers. The peaks of these ranges form the one region of Western Australia which can occasionally experience a dusting of snow in the winter months.

Travelling north, the rugged and fertile Great Southern region gives way to the wide curving landscapes and wheat fields of the Wheatbelt. Vistas of golden wheat waving and whispering in the wind, prosperous farms, lively small towns, and more of the state's spectacular wildflowers — particularly the pink and white everlastings — provide a great contrast with the scenery of the Great Southern. Some

unusual rock formations can be found here and the most spectacular of these is Wave Rock close to the small town of Hyden. This formation of weathered granite — sandy yellow, through a pinky cream to streaks of dark brown and steel grey — is shaped like a towering wave rising more than 15 metres above ground and stretching for a full 100 metres.

Closer to Perth the golden landscapes of the wheat fields are replaced by the greenery of the Avon Valley with its fertile pastures, wooded hills and fast-flowing streams. In

winter the Avon attracts whitewater rafters and canoeists, and in summer its gentle waters help to cool the green and shady woodlands. The Avon Valley was one of the first areas explored by Captain Stirling's men in the establishment of the Swan River Colony and many beautiful farms and homesteads in the area date back to those first days of settlement. Northam is the major town of the region — a thriving agricultural centre and the home of the state's only white swans, which have lived there since their introduction from England nearly 100 years ago. Many of the beautiful houses and public buildings nearby, in the historic town of York, were built by convicts and have been lovingly maintained and restored. York is known for its many festivals, the most popular of these being the October Jazz Festival and the August Vintage and Veteran Car Race.

On the fringes of the Avon Valley is New Norcia — a peaceful and gracious cameo of Spanish architecture in the green hills and fields of wildflowers north-east of Perth. This Spanish Benedictine mission was established in 1846 and is still owned and occupied by the Benedictine monks. A rustic and beautiful abbey church built from mud plaster, tree trunks and local stones houses the tomb of the founder, Dom Rosendo Salvado, and the present-day monks still make their exotic liqueur and bake delicious sourdough bread and other delicacies in the old bakehouse.

Easily accessible from Perth, the Avon Valley, the Midlands and the Great Southern form a region of colour and variety sustained by agriculture, wheat, tourism, viticulture and, in more recent years, a growing industry in cultivated flowers.

LEFT   Extensive pastures fill the landscape between New Norcia and Perth.
BELOW   The college chapel at New Norcia — established as a Benedictine mission in 1846, the monastery is still home to Benedictine monks.
FOLLOWING PAGES   The glorious still waters off Esperance can quickly change to massive waves capped with foaming white water.

ABOVE The Jetty on the Torndirrup coastline between Albany and Esperance is a favoured spot for watching the sunset.
RIGHT The Natural Bridge at Torndirrup National Park spans the wild waters of the Southern Ocean.
OPPOSITE The Gap, in Torndirrup National Park, is a popular site with ecotourists for whale watching.

BRIG AMITY

Majestically overlooking Albany's Princess Royal Harbour is the *Brig Amity*, a replica of the twin-masted, square-rigged sailing vessel which brought the first European settlers to this southernmost tip of Western Australia. The original *Brig Amity* was built in Canada and had been an Atlantic trader before she was sold to the new colonial government in Sydney in 1824 for use as a supply vessel.

On 9 November 1826, under the command of Major Edmund Lockyer, the *Brig Amity* set sail from Sydney to form a new settlement on the west coast of Australia. In addition to the regular crew and master she was carrying a surgeon, a storekeeper and quartermaster, an army sergeant and captain, with 18 soldiers, and 23 convict tradesmen. There were also sheep, pigs and all the other supplies thought essential for establishing a new settlement. The voyage was fairly uneventful apart from some stormy weather in the Bass Strait and the constant fear that the convicts might mutiny and overwhelm the crew and the military. The *Brig Amity* sailed into Princess Royal Harbour on Christmas Day 1826.

In 1972 Mavis Watterson, an Albany resident, suggested that a replica should be built in time to celebrate the 150th anniversary of the *Brig Amity*'s arrival. A local committee was formed and, with research by a local historian, Les Johnson, and boatbuilder, Stan Austin, the replica was completed in time for Christmas 1976. The *Brig Amity* replica is fully fitted inside and out in faithful duplication of the original ship.

As well as her vital role in the settlement of Albany, the *Brig Amity* was used in the establishment of a settlement at Moreton Bay in Queensland. She was wrecked off Flinders Island in 1845.

RIGHT This stretch of Scenic Loop Road, a 36-kilometre road around the coast, offers a drive of spectacular beauty.

BELOW The coastal town of Albany offers magnificent views, natural rock formations, splendid bays and beaches, and a rich sea-faring history.

OPPOSITE The perfect wave! One hundred metres long and 15 metres high, Wave Rock near Hyden is a breathtaking wave of solid rock striped in rich.bands of colour created by iron hydroxide and carbonates.

FOLLOWING PAGES The Stirling Range is a single row of peaks which is 65 kilometres long and 10 kilometres wide. The colours here range from reds through to purples, and the area is notable for its collection of unusual native and endemic plants.

The Goldfields
and the Nullarbor

The West Australian gold rush was one of the biggest in Australia's history and today, more than 100 years later, the world's largest single open-cut mining operation continues to recover gold at Kalgoorlie–Boulder on the world-famous Golden Mile. The gold rush began here in 1893 when Paddy Hannan, Tom Flannigan and Daniel O'Shea discovered gold at Mt Charlotte — a small hill close to what is now Kalgoorlie. Within a few months 100 leases had been pegged and miners and prospectors arrived on foot, on horses and camels, and in ramshackle carts, to make their homes in shacks constructed from hessian or old packing cases. The population of the region grew as the fame of the Golden Mile spread, and in only a few years 30 000 people had settled in Kalgoorlie and a fine town had been established. The wealth of the region was reflected in the town's gracious and substantial public buildings, and the thirst of the inhabitants was catered for by 93 pubs! By 1896 the rail link to Perth was operating, and between 1897 and 1903 hundreds of mining companies were floated and the mining and investment boom reached its peak. The Golden Mile became the richest square mile of gold-bearing ore in the world and today produces in excess of $310 million dollars worth of gold every year.

With the surge of gold seekers to the area other sites revealed rich ore deposits and townsites developed at Southern Cross, Coolgardie, Norseman and Kambalda. Other towns roared to life in the boom and were gone again as soon as the gold was

PREVIOUS PAGES Kalgoorlie appeared seemingly overnight. Gold was discovered in 1893 and within just a few years the town's population had reached 30 000.
LEFT Even the arid conditions of the gold-fields can support wildflowers!

exhausted. Within a period of 10 years the populations of these towns had grown to as many as 10 000 and then slumped until they were abandoned. Towns bigger than Kalgoorlie were left ghost towns — bleak pockets of a proud history scattered across the desert, and there they remain, eerie in their isolation but still able to capture the imagination with the tales of hardship and endeavour, villainy and glittering success which surround them.

It was a harsh and brutal life on the goldfields and hundreds of miners died from injury and disease. In this riverless semi-desert water was at a premium and the Goldfields Water Scheme, which brought water by pipeline from near Perth, enabled the region to develop. The rugged history of the gold-fields is still reflected in the life of the region and the character of its people whose down-to-earth manner and gritty determination enables them to cope with the blistering heat and isolation.

At the heart of the region the twin towns of Kalgoorlie–Boulder have ample evidence of their wealthy and historic past and their present flourishing economy. Beautifully restored Victorian buildings with wide verandahs and wrought-iron lace work border the broad streets. Flowering eucalypts, sandal-wood trees, hibiscus, bottlebrush, the famous Sturt's desert pea and the brilliant yellow of the wattle bring bursts of colour to gardens and parks, and while the mines continue to supply gold to the international market the industry's history is captured in the Goldfields Museum and many other small museums and tourist mines.

The rainfall here is sparse and erratic, the network of inland lakes largely dried out, and when rain does fall it is fast absorbed into the parched ground. Dingoes, emus, rabbits and kangaroos make their homes in this country, and crows, bustards and eagles watch for their prey while cockatoos and parrots dart with flashes of brilliant colour through the trees. The racehorse goanna can be found here — dragon-like, swift and watchful, it merges so effectively into the background that its sudden dramatic movement is all the more shocking.

The region north of Kalgoorlie is ghost-town country but there are many other small inhabited towns rich in history and alive with the true spirit of the outback still remaining. Eucalypts, salmon gums and blackbutt trees rise from the flat and dry land, but the arrival of a little winter rain can bring great stretches of wildflowers to bloom in all their colourful glory. To the south, the busy town of Kambalda, its gold long exhausted, is now a thriving centre for the mining of nickel. Gold is still mined at Norseman — the town which stands sentinel at the start of the Eyre Highway.

Norseman is the last urban centre before the great barren tract of the Nullarbor Plain. *Null arbor* means 'no trees', however, for most of the more than 850 kilometres of the Eyre Highway, until it reaches the border with South Australia, trees are a constant though unimpressive feature of the land-scape. The long, straight Eyre Highway is the work of Edward John Eyre, who crossed the continent in 1841 on a five-month journey which defined the route for the highway. The road runs along the edge of the Nullarbor, close to the high coastal cliffs of the Great Australian Bight which plunge abruptly to the water below.

The Nullarbor is a vast and ancient limestone plateau with a huge network of underground caves and passages, sinkholes and blowholes. The above-ground landscape is stark and challenging — endless horizons of dusty red scrub give way to vast luminous white sand dunes rippled by the winds, dead trees reach upwards bleached white like bones against the endless blue of the sky. Old stone fences and half-buried abandoned buildings add to the haunting mystery of the landscape. At Eucla, just 12 kilometres from the South Australian border, the original weather and telegraph repeater stations are almost submerged by the dunes, except for a few weeks each year when a change in the wind shifts the sand and uncovers the buildings. This is the eastern point of farewell to Western Australia — a dazzling spectacle of rolling sandhills shifting and whispering with the ocean winds.

ABOVE AND LEFT· A century ago Broad Arrow boasted a population of over 2000, eight hotels, a stock exchange and a hospital. Today, the wild times of the gold rush long past, it has a permanent population of around 20. The Broad Arrow Tavern, built in 1896, is the last pub in town. OPPOSITE Gwalia is another mining town since abandoned. Today it is most famous as a temporary workplace of former United States President Herbert Hoover.

TOP AND ABOVE Site of the greatest gold rush in Western Australia, Kalgoorlie proved to be the location of the richest gold seam in Australia — the famous Golden Mile. Unlike many gold rush towns, Kalgoorlie is still the centre of a thriving mining community. RIGHT The old post office in the town of Cue.

BRINGING WATER TO THE GOLDFIELDS

Gold fever brought thousands of people to the goldfields at the end of the last century. While individual fortunes were made and lost it was Western Australia itself which was the greatest winner. The 1890s gold rush put Western Australia on the map and today it is still home to a hugely profitable and thriving goldmining industry. It is doubtful that the industry could have survived, however, without the genius of Charles O'Connor — the engineer whose ambitious plan for a pipeline succeeded in bringing desperately needed water to the goldfields.

At the end of the 19th century, West Australian Premier Sir John Forrest spoke of his dream for a stream of fresh water for the region and promised a solution, but it was Charles O'Connor's vision and commitment which made that promise a reality. While others debated the possibilities of sinking artesian wells or pumping sea water from Esperance, O'Connor produced a plan to build a massive reservoir at Mundaring — a gorge in the Darling Range east of Perth. Water would be pumped from Mundaring through a 563-kilometre pipeline to the goldfields. This involved not only extraordinary distance but also the problem of pumping water uphill — Kalgoorlie is 400 metres higher than Mundaring. Premier Forrest backed the scheme, but during the course of its construction the pipeline project was under constant attack. The cost, in excess of two million pounds, was widely criticised and O'Connor was hounded on all sides by sceptics, politicians, newspapers and competitors. Driven to despair by his critics, Charles O'Connor shot himself in 1902, just months before the opening of the pipeline in January 1903.

The Goldfields Water Scheme still supplies water to the region and the story of its construction and its social, political and economic impact can be seen in the C Y O'Connor Pipeline Museum at Mundaring.

TOP Built in 1877 to link Perth with the eastern states the Eucla telegraph station was abandoned in 1929 and has since been reclaimed and buried by the desert sands.

ABOVE When travelling from the east across the Nullarbor Plain, Norseman and nearby Lake Cowan are the first signs of major human settlement to be seen.

OPPOSITE The soaring cliffs of the Great Australian Bight provide a dramatic end to the flat monotony of the Nullarbor Plain.

FOLLOWING PAGES The overwhelming beauty of the West Australian landscape — in all its diversity and vivid colours — makes the state truly a land of contrasts.

INDEX